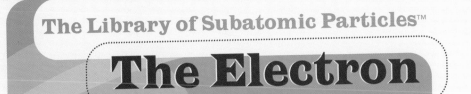

The Library of Subatomic Particles™

The Electron

Fred Bortz

The Rosen Publishing Group, Inc., New York

To Susan, for the electricity she brings to my life

Published in 2004 by The Rosen Publishing Group, Inc.
29 East 21st Street, New York, NY 10010

Library of Congress Cataloging-in-Publication Data

Bortz, Alfred B.
The electron / Fred Bortz. — 1st ed.
        p. cm. — (The library of subatomic particles)
Includes bibliographical references and index.
Summary: Presents the story of the discovery of the first subatomic particle and how it revolutionized understanding of the atom in chemistry and led to the new field of electronics.
ISBN 0-8239-4528-6 (lib. bdg.)
1. Electrons—Juvenile literature. [1. Electrons.] I. Title. II. Series.
QC793.5.E62B67 2004
539.7'2112—dc21

                                        2003007043

Manufactured in the United States of America

On the cover: an artist's illustration of electrons in orbit around an atomic nucleus

Contents

Introduction

The story of the electron, the tiny bit of matter at the heart of much of modern technology, begins with a very old question. About 2,500 years ago, the Greek philosophers Democritus and Leucippus asked, "What is matter made of?" They imagined cutting a piece of matter in half, then cutting one of its halves in half, then cutting one of those pieces in half, and so on until the resulting pieces could no longer be cut. The last pieces would be indivisible, or *atomos* in Greek. Democritus's atoms turned out to be similar to what we call molecules today. A water molecule, two hydrogen atoms combined with one oxygen atom, is not indivisible, but it is the smallest speck of matter that can still be called water.

Hydrogen and oxygen are examples of substances that scientists call elements. In a pure element, all the atoms are the same. Scientists classify water as a compound, a substance with more than one kind of atom but with all its atoms combined into the same kind of molecules. The science of chemistry deals with the way atoms and molecules interact, react, and combine.

If molecules can be divided into atoms, it is natural to ask if atoms can also be divided. And if so, might we look into the atom to understand why only certain combinations of atoms form molecules? A little over a century ago, physicists began to answer those questions. As they probed inside atoms, they gained a deeper understanding of not only the chemical behavior of matter but also other phenomena like electricity, magnetism, and light.

This book tells the story of the electron— the first subatomic particle to be discovered— the knowledge that people have gained from studying it, and the many useful devices that have resulted from that knowledge.

Chapter One

The Discovery of the Electron

When twenty-four-year-old Joseph John Thomson joined the world-famous Cavendish Laboratory at Britain's Cambridge University in 1881, the atmosphere there was "electric" in more ways than one. Thomson hoped to follow in the footsteps of the laboratory's founder, James Clerk Maxwell, who was famous for his set of equations that not only described the relationship between electricity and magnetism but also predicted waves of energy that travel through space at very high speeds.

Astonishingly, the calculated speed of those electromagnetic waves turned out to match the speed of light. Maxwell's clever mathematics had unified electricity, magnetism, and light into a single natural phenomenon: electromagnetism. By Thomson's time, chemists had evidence that matter was composed of what were thought to be indivisible atoms and that atoms combined in particular ways to form molecules. They also had discovered that electricity was related to chemical reactions.

Thomson wanted to use his mathematical gifts to make discoveries about the electrical nature of matter. His boss, John William Strutt, more commonly known as

Joseph John (J. J.) Thomson. Though awkward with laboratory equipment, Thomson used his brilliant insight to become one of the greatest experimental scientists of his time. In 1897, he announced the discovery of the first known subatomic particle, which we now call the electron.

Baron Rayleigh, had other plans. Rayleigh, who became the second Cavendish professor of experimental physics in 1879 after Maxwell's death, believed that in physics mathematical skills should not stand alone. If J. J. Thomson intended to work at Cavendish, he would have to do more than calculation. He would have to work in the laboratory!

Unfortunately, Thomson was less than skillful with scientific apparatus. His contributions to experiments were more of the mind than of the hand. "J. J. was very awkward with his fingers, and I found it very necessary not to encourage him to handle the instruments!" said H. F. Newell, Thomson's assistant in his early years at the lab. "But he was very helpful in talking over the ways in which he thought things ought to go."

So Much Electricity, So Little Mass

Thomson's most important investigations were into the well-known but poorly understood phenomenon of cathode rays. Today's familiar cathode ray tubes (CRTs), such as those used for computer monitors and television picture tubes, are a far cry from the first CRTs. As early as the 1830s, scientists were experimenting with the electrical behavior of gases in glass tubes with two electrodes inserted at opposite ends. They needed low pressure for their experiments, so they pumped hard on the tubes to draw out most of the gas before sealing them. The

Thomson's Cathode Ray Apparatus. Now on display at the Science Museum in South Kensington, London, these glass tubes containing electrodes enabled J. J. Thomson to determine that cathode rays were streams of negatively charged particles with a mass that was only a tiny fraction of that of the hydrogen atom, the smallest known particle up to that time.

invention of a better vacuum pump in 1855 made it possible to remove nearly all the gas, and things began to get very interesting when electricity was applied. The remaining gas would glow, especially near the negative electrode, or cathode.

When Thomson began studying cathode rays, scientists knew that the cathode was shooting

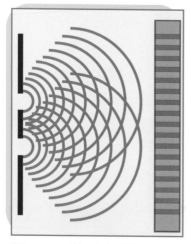

Wave or Particle? In a famous experiment in 1803, Thomas Young split a narrow beam of light into two parts and produced an "interference pattern," a series of light and dark bands characteristic of a wave phenomenon, rather than the two bright spots that would be expected if light were a stream of particles. J. J. Thomson explored the same question about cathode rays.

out tiny negatively charged particles, but they were divided about whether the particles themselves were the cathode rays or whether the glow resulted from waves that the particles produced. Thomson hoped to settle the question with an experiment, just as Thomas Young had done in 1801 when similar arguments swirled about the nature of light.

Young's experiment demonstrated that light was a wave phenomenon by producing the interference patterns that were characteristic of waves. For cathode rays, however, the experimental results had so far been mixed. So Thomson kept an open mind and began by repeating what others had done.

He applied magnetic fields to the tubes, and the rays curved in the direction that the magnetic field would cause negatively charged particles to curve. But when he passed the beam between a pair of oppositely charged electrified plates, the cathode rays went straight through, producing a glowing spot at the center of the glass. If cathode rays were streams of negative particles, the glowing spot on the glass should have been offset in the direction of the positively charged plate—but it wasn't.

Thomson then devised three new experiments. In the first, he put an electrometer, a device that measures electrical charge, into the tube. When the glow struck the electrometer, the device indicated a large negative charge. When the glow just missed, the electrometer measured very little charge. Thus cathode rays were either a stream of negative charges, or they carried such a stream with them.

Thomson's second experiment clarified the puzzling results with the electrified plates. He reasoned that an energetic beam of negative particles would electrify the gas it passed through and the charged gas atoms would drift toward the oppositely charged plate, neutralizing the electric field within the tube. Thomson believed that if he could do a better job of

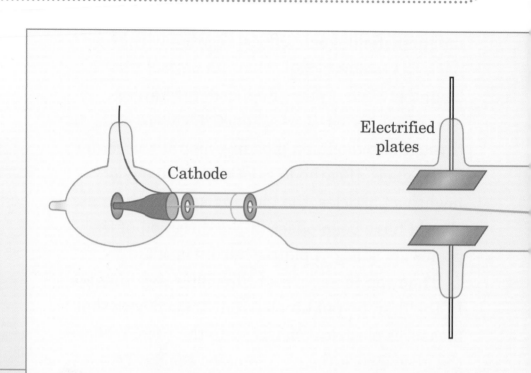

Cathode

Electrified plates

Thomson's Second Experiment. J. J. Thomson demonstrated that cathode rays were negatively charged particles by repeating earlier experiments with a better vacuum pump. In those experiments, the beam passed straight through a pair of electrified plates because a small amount of gas remaining in the tube became electrified and cancelled the field between the plates. In the better vacuum with almost no gas, that didn't happen, and the beam deflected toward the positively charged plate as shown here.

removing the residual gas from the tube, there would be too few molecules to neutralize the electric field. He got the best available vacuum pump and tried the experiment again. Sure enough, the cathode rays now deflected toward the positive plate. Thomson was now confident that they were negatively charged "corpuscles,"

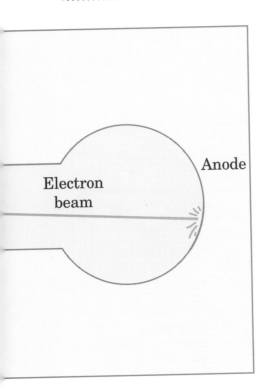

Electron beam

Anode

that is, particles, shot from the cathode.

The second experiment also enabled Thomson to measure the speed of those tiny particles. He added a magnet to the apparatus. The magnetic force on the corpuscles depended on their speed, but the electrical force did not. Thomson arranged the fields so that the magnetic and electrical forces were in opposite directions, then he adjusted the fields until the particles went straight, indicating that the forces were equal. Knowing that, he was able to compute the speed from the strength of the two fields.

Thomson was then ready for a final experiment that would allow him to compute the corpuscles' electric charge compared to their mass. He allowed just enough gas back into a tube so that the cathode rays' glowing path could be seen and measured precisely. He

13

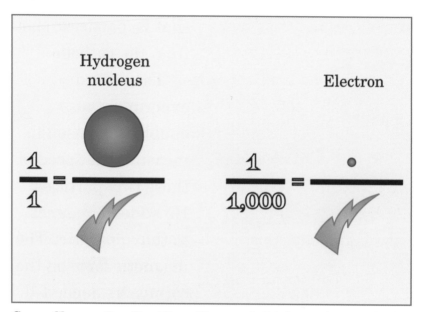

Same Charge, Smaller Mass. Thomson's third experiment, which measured the charge-to-mass ratio of the "corpuscles" in cathode rays, produced a very surprising result. That ratio was more than 1,000 times as large for the negatively charged corpuscles as for a positively charged atom of hydrogen. (More precise measurements have since revealed a ratio of approximately 1,837-to-1.) Since nature seemed to have a basic unit of charge, the most likely explanation was that corpuscles were subatomic particles with only a small fraction of the mass of hydrogen atoms.

applied a magnetic field and measured the curvature of the path. Knowing the speed, the curvature, and the formula for magnetic force, he was able to use his results to measure the charge-to-mass ratio of the corpuscles.

He discovered that the charge-to-mass ratio was about 1,000 times as large for these corpuscles as for an electrically charged hydrogen atom, the lightest particle known at that time. For that to be true, the corpuscles either had to carry a lot of charge or have very little mass. Other scientists' measurements indicated that there was a basic minimum unit of electric charge for both positive and negative electricity, so Thomson assumed that each negative corpuscle and each positive hydrogen atom carried the same amount of electrical charge. That meant that the corpuscle had only a thousandth of the mass of the tiny hydrogen atom. Today, we know more precisely that this particle's mass is only 1/1,837.15 of the hydrogen atom.

The result was astounding. Cathode rays were beams of particles, as Thomson had suspected all along, but their mass was far smaller than he could have imagined. In his 1906 Nobel Prize lecture, Thomson still called the particles "corpuscles." But he realized their importance went far beyond cathode rays, stating, "The corpuscle appears to form a part of all kinds of matter under the most diverse conditions; it seems natural therefore to regard it as one of the bricks of which atoms are built up."

Chapter Two

Electrons, Atoms, and Light

In science, finding the answer to one question leads to many more. If atoms are not indivisible, as J. J. Thomson's work had demonstrated, then what other subatomic particles are there besides electrons? How do electrons and those other subatomic particles fit together to make different kinds of atoms, and how are subatomic parts related to the properties of whole atoms?

By Thomson's time, chemists had identified some rules of nature that seemed to govern the way atoms combine to form molecules, and they were beginning to recognize that those rules were related to the number of electrons in the combining atoms. But they wondered why those particular rules applied and others didn't. They thought that knowledge of subatomic particles like the electron might provide the key.

From Plum Pudding to the Nucleus

J. J. Thomson put forward an educated guess about the internal structure of atoms. Since electrons carry so little mass, he envisioned the positively charged bulk of atoms as a kind of pudding containing tiny electron plums.

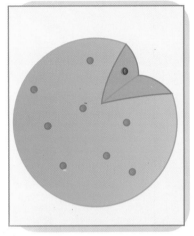

Atoms for Dessert? If atoms have tiny electrons, what is the rest of their structure like? Thomson proposed a model based on a popular English dessert, plum pudding. He envisioned the atom as a uniform bulk of positive charge with tiny negatively charged electron "plums" scattered throughout.

Though Thomson's plum pudding model seemed sensible, no one tested it until Ernest Rutherford came up with a way to probe matter with radioactive beams. Born in New Zealand in 1871, Rutherford first explored radioactivity as Thomson's student in the Cavendish Laboratory between 1895 and 1898. He quickly discovered two distinct forms of radioactivity and named them "alpha rays" and "beta rays" after the first two letters of the Greek alphabet.

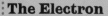
Radioactive material

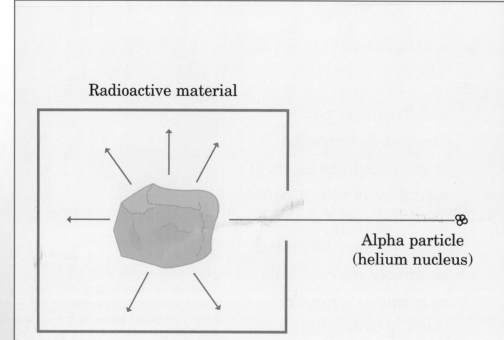

Alpha particle
(helium nucleus)

Rutherford Discovers the Atomic Nucleus. Ernest Rutherford used alpha particles emitted from radioactive substances as tiny bullets to probe the structure of the atom. Rutherford shot the alpha particles at a thin sheet of metal foil. Most of the alpha particles went straight through or deflected only slightly. However, a few alphas deflected far off to the side or even backward. From the pattern of scattering, Rutherford deduced that most of the atom was empty space and nearly all of its mass and all of its positive charge were in a very compact nucleus at its center.

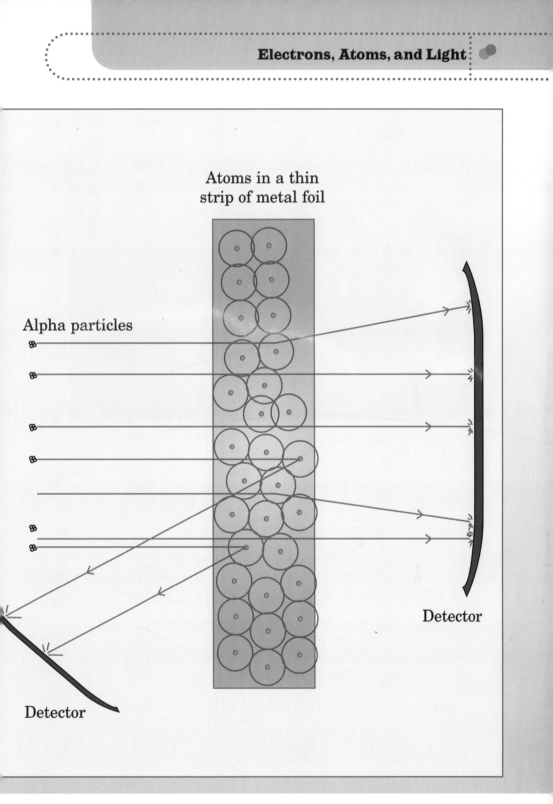

Atoms in a thin
strip of metal foil

Alpha particles

Detector

Detector

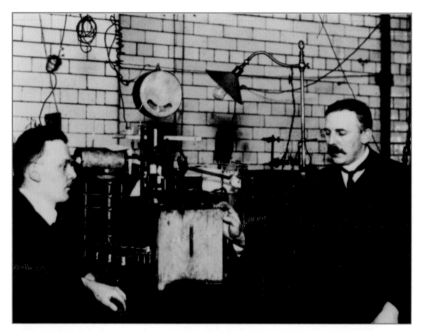

Rutherford and Geiger. Rutherford's discovery of the nucleus would not have been possible without the contributions of his students. Shown here in their Manchester University laboratory are Rutherford *(left)* and Hans Geiger, who devised a very sensitive instrument to detect and count alpha particles. Ernest Marsden, using Geiger's detectors, discovered alphas that had been scattered through unexpectedly large angles.

When Rutherford finished his work at Cambridge, he took a faculty position at McGill University in Montreal, Canada, where he and his colleague Frederick Soddy discovered "gamma rays," a third form of radioactivity, in 1902. They also discovered that alpha and beta radiation were streams of fast-moving particles of opposite electric charges. The alphas were positively charged and much more massive than the negatively charged betas. (We now know that beta rays are electrons.) Rutherford returned to England in 1907 as a professor at the University of Manchester, full of ideas about how to apply his discoveries.

Rutherford planned to shoot a beam of alpha particles through a thin sheet of metal foil and measure how the alphas deflected, or scattered, as they interacted with atoms in the foil. By studying alpha scattering carefully, he hoped to be able to determine the size, spacing, and perhaps even the shape of the atoms in the foil. First, he needed to know more about the alpha "bullets" he was shooting, and he needed ways to keep track of them. By 1908, his student, Hans Geiger, had devised an instrument to detect and count alpha particles. The two researchers then quickly confirmed Rutherford's suspicion that alpha particles were helium atoms without their electrons.

The next year, 1909, they began their scattering experiments. Would the plum pudding model be proven correct, or would they find, as some people expected, evidence that atoms were hard little balls? Nearly all the alphas passed

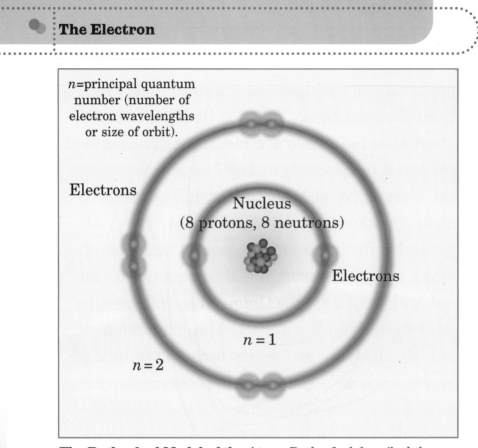

n=principal quantum number (number of electron wavelengths or size of orbit).

Electrons

Nucleus
(8 protons, 8 neutrons)

Electrons

$n = 1$

$n = 2$

The Rutherford Model of the Atom. Rutherford described the atom as a miniature planetary system—mainly empty space with most of the mass concentrated in its compact central nucleus. The electrical force plays the role of gravity, holding light "planets"— electrons—in their orbits. That model raised some questions that were later resolved by replacing planetary orbits with "shells" containing certain numbers of electrons, as shown here in this modern depiction of an oxygen atom.

straight through the foil or were deflected only slightly. If the atoms were hard balls, Rutherford and Geiger would have expected more deflection. It was beginning to look as if Thomson's model was right, but the researchers needed more detailed measurements to be certain.

Rutherford also needed to clarify one puzzling result. A few alpha particles were unaccounted for. He wondered if the missing particles had been deflected so much that they missed the detectors. If so, what was scattering those few alphas through such large angles while most passed nearly straight through the foil?

Always intrigued by unlikely results, but not wanting to divert Geiger from his detailed measurements, Rutherford assigned the task of looking for large-angle scattering to Ernest Marsden, a young student just learning the techniques of research. Marsden found the missing alpha particles, and a great surprise. Some alpha particles scattered to the left or right of the original detectors, and a few even scattered backward!

Rutherford described this result as "almost as incredible as if you had fired a 15-inch shell at a piece of tissue-paper and it came back and hit you." Rutherford published his findings in 1911, explaining his results with a new model of the atom.

In Rutherford's picture, an atom was like a miniature solar system with electrical forces playing the role of gravity. The atom is mostly empty space, and most of its mass is concentrated in a very small, positively charged central body called the nucleus. In orbit around that minuscule sun are much tinier negatively charged "planets," the electrons.

This model made sense of both Geiger's and Marsden's results. Because the atoms were mostly empty space, most alpha particles passed through the foil without coming very close to a nucleus, and thus they scattered very little. On rare occasions, a fast-moving alpha particle made a nearly direct hit on a nucleus, which in the metals Rutherford used was much more massive than the alpha, and it scattered the alpha sideways or even backward.

A Puzzle in the Light

Rutherford's model raised new questions. According to Maxwell's equations, an electrically charged body moving along a curve must radiate energy in the form of electromagnetic waves. Thus, orbiting electrons in atoms should be constantly glowing and losing energy, and that would cause them to spiral inward toward the nucleus. It wouldn't be long before the

Planck and Bohr. This photograph shows Niels Bohr *(left)* and Max Planck, two pioneers of quantum physics. In 1900, Planck invented the quantum as a mathematical device to fix a problem in his theory of the spectrum of hot bodies, but it turned out to have a real physical meaning that blurred the distinction between electromagnetic waves and particles. Bohr applied the same blurring to electrons in atoms and came up with a theory that resolved problems with Rutherford's planetary model of atoms.

nucleus consumed its electron planets altogether. If the planetary model was correct, then the laws of electromagnetism, or the laws of motion—or both—must be wrong, at least when they are examined at the atomic scale.

The research that would resolve this problem had, in fact, already been done and had produced equally puzzling results. In 1895, the renowned professor Max Planck at the University of Berlin in Germany had just turned his theoretical skills to a new problem. Could he come up with a formula that described the spectrum, the different colors of light that radiated from hot bodies?

Planck had plenty of experimental data to work with. Scientists heated furnaces and observed the light that came from holes in their sides. Using a spectrometer, a device that spreads light into its component colors like a prism, they had produced graphs showing the brightness of each color in the glow. On the graph, each color was represented by a corresponding frequency, the rate at which the electromagnetic wave wiggles. For visible light, red has the lowest frequency and violet has the highest. The measurements went from infrared (below red) through ultraviolet (above violet) at higher temperatures.

At all temperatures, the graphs had a common appearance. Going from infrared to ultraviolet, they would rise to a peak and then drop off to zero. Higher temperatures produced more intense light, so the peaks of the graph went higher. The peak also shifted toward higher frequencies as the temperature rose, corresponding to the changing color that the experimenters could observe. But no matter how high the temperature, the measured intensity always rose to a peak, then dropped off sharply at higher frequencies.

Planck developed a mathematical model of a hot, radiating body as a collection of vibrating atoms, each producing electromagnetic waves. The sum of those waves produced a calculated spectrum, which he graphed. His method produced a remarkable match to actual data at the low-frequency end, but it failed miserably in the ultraviolet region. Instead of reaching a peak and then dropping off, Planck's model produced an ever-rising light intensity at high frequencies, an ultraviolet catastrophe for his model.

Then Planck hit on a mathematical trick. His original model allowed each atomic vibration to have any amount of energy, no matter how small, as if energy were a liquid that you could measure out in any amount. Planck replaced that model with one in which energy came in discrete bits like grains of sand. He called the unit of energy a quantum. The vibrations could carry zero, one, two, or three quanta of energy and so forth. But they could not have any fractions, such as one third of a quantum or two and one-half quanta.

Planck realized that if the quanta were small, they wouldn't affect his results much. You can measure out almost exactly any volume of very fine sand that you'd like. But if the quanta were large, like a pile of pebbles instead of fine grains of sand, then many of the energy values possible in his original model could not be achieved in the new one. If he had fine grains at low frequencies and large grains at high frequencies, he could eliminate the ultraviolet catastrophe. To make that happen, Planck kept the ratio between the quantum's energy and frequency the same. If the frequency was twice as large, the quantum had to be twice as big. Triple the frequency, and the quantum's energy also tripled, and so on.

The ultraviolet catastrophe disappeared. By adjusting the ratio, Planck was able to make the peaks of his graphs match the peaks from actual experiments. But that was not all. Astonishingly, there was one special ratio that made the calculated intensity match the measured values not just at the peaks, but at all frequencies and all temperatures. Planck published his results in

1900. He knew that his mathematical trick and the ratio he had discovered were telling him something about physics, but he didn't understand the message.

The Photoelectric Effect

Ultraviolet light also played a role in another puzzling phenomenon. When J. J. Thomson spoke of finding electrons in many circumstances in his 1906 Nobel Prize lecture, he included the photoelectric effect, in which a beam of light could knock electrons out of certain metals. To release electrons, each metal has a particular "threshold" frequency. Below that frequency, the metal does not give up its electrons, no matter how intense, or bright, the light. Above that frequency, even the dimmest light would free some electrons. For most metals, that threshold was in the violet or ultraviolet range. But why should there be a threshold frequency at all?

The threshold question was answered in a paper written in 1905 by a little-known patent clerk in Switzerland named Albert Einstein. Einstein knew that the amount of energy needed to free an electron varied from one metal to another. He realized that if Planck's quanta were

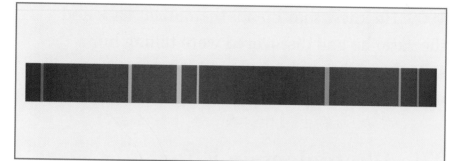

The Emission Spectrum of Hydrogen. Unlike the continuous spectrum of a hot body that glows in all wavelengths, excited atoms of each element produce line spectra like this one, glowing with certain frequencies of light and not others. Niels Bohr's atomic theory stated that nature permitted only certain energy levels for orbiting electrons, which would then emit light quanta when they dropped from one energy level to a lower one. His theory's predictions matched the line spectrum of hydrogen perfectly.

not merely mathematical conveniences but real particles, which he called photons, they might be responsible for the photoelectric threshold. Einstein explained that photons are not like individuals who can gang up for a greater push. Either a photon has enough energy to knock out an electron all by itself, or the electron stays put.

Photons below the frequency threshold simply lack the energy needed to knock electrons free, no matter how many there are. Above the frequency threshold, even a single photon has enough energy to free an electron, so even the dimmest light of that color can free electrons.

Thanks to Young's experiment, everyone had thought that light was not a stream of particles, but a series of waves. Maxwell's equations had identified the waves as electromagnetic. The case seemed closed, but Einstein's work was calling for a new trial. Now light seemed to be made of waves in some circumstances and particles in others! How could that be?

The first steps toward an answer came from Danish physicist Niels Bohr, who was looking for a solution to Rutherford's unstable planetary model of the atom and had begun to study the spectra of electrically excited gases. These gases had very different spectra from the continuous bands of color produced by a hot furnace. When the light from such gases was spread into a spectrum, each gas produced a distinct series of bright lines. The glowing gas radiated at certain frequencies but not others. The hydrogen spectrum in particular had a few sets of frequencies that fit recognizable mathematical relationships.

Bohr made some shrewd guesses about electrons in atoms, which he hoped would provide insight into the spectra. He began by accepting French physicist Louis-Victor de Broglie's unusual interpretation of Einstein's theory of photoelectricity. If light waves could have particle characteristics, de Broglie

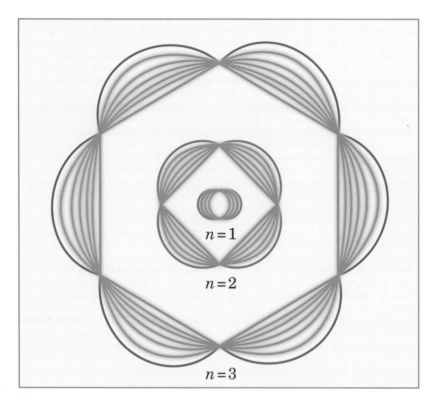

$n=1$

$n=2$

$n=3$

Electron Waves in Atoms. Bohr's atomic theory relied on a formula of Louis-Victor de Broglie, who applied Planck's formula for light quanta to compute the wavelength for a particle that has a particular energy. Applying that formula to electrons, Bohr came up with a set of allowed orbits in which the electron's wavelength would fit around the orbit an exact number of times. Since a wave has two halves that are reflections of each other, one with a crest and the other with a trough, this diagram shows the orbits corresponding to one, two, and three electron wavelengths.

suggested, then subatomic particles could have the characteristics of waves.

Bohr began with de Broglie's formula for the wavelength of electrons, which was related to their energy. Then he proposed that orbiting electrons did not radiate at all if the distance around their orbits was an exact number of wavelengths. Just as musical instruments have certain natural frequencies in which they sustain tones, electron waves in atoms have certain natural orbits, each with its own energy level. Bohr proposed that when an electron drops from one orbit to another with lower energy, the energy difference appears as a photon. Bohr calculated the frequencies of light that would result from hydrogen's natural orbits, and the results matched the observed lines in the hydrogen spectrum.

With Bohr's insight, the planetary model of the atom was making more sense. It required scientists to revamp some of their most basic ideas, including eliminating the sharp distinction between particles and waves. The theory of the quantum was about to set off a revolution in scientific thought and lead to technologies that no one could have imagined a few years earlier. At the heart of that revolution would be a tiny speck of negative charge, the electron.

Chapter Three

Electrons and Chemistry

Now that the distinction between particles and waves had blurred, physicists struggled to find new ways to understand the laws of motion within the atom. Among them was Erwin Schrödinger, who developed an equation that described a particle's position by a mathematical formula called a wave function. Schrödinger's equation launched a new field of physics called quantum mechanics. Strangely, a particle was no longer considered to be at an exact place. Rather, the particle's wave function gave the probability of finding it in many different places.

To understand what that means, imagine an object bouncing back and forth so fast on a very tight spring that all you can see is a blur. Near the ends of its bounces, the object moves more slowly and the blur is less blurry. So where is it? It could be anywhere along the path, but it is more likely to be near one of the less blurry ends than in the blurry middle. In quantum mechanics, the blur is the object.

When Schrödinger applied his equation to the hydrogen atom, it produced a series of different electron wave functions, each concentrated at a certain distance from the nucleus and each having a certain energy. The distances and energies were the same ones that Bohr had calculated.

Dmitry Ivanovich Mendeleyev. In 1869, Mendeleyev devised an arrangement of rows and columns that he called the periodic table of the elements. It demonstrated the regularity of their chemical properties, though he could not explain the reason for that pattern, which we now know is due to the quantum nature of matter.

Why the Periodic Table Is Periodic

As physicists looked more deeply, they discovered that quantum mechanics could also explain one

Erwin Schrödinger.
Schrödinger devised a famous equation that combined the quantum nature of matter and energy with the laws of force and motion, launching a new field of physics known as quantum mechanics.

of chemistry's great mysteries—what underlies the regularity of the periodic table of elements discovered by the Russian chemist Dmitry Ivanovich Mendeleyev in 1869.

Mendeleyev had arranged the known elements by increasing atomic weight into rows and columns. All the elements in a vertical column formed similar compounds. For example, sodium is above potassium in column I, and both form molecules with one atom of chlorine. Their neighboring atoms in column II, magnesium and calcium, form molecules containing two chlorine atoms. After the electron was discovered, it soon became apparent that the different number of electrons in atoms had something to do with their placement in Mendeleyev's columns. But it took quantum mechanics to reveal the explanation.

According to Schrödinger, each electron orbit in an atom could be labeled by a quantum number called n that was equal to the number of electron wavelengths that fit into that orbit. Physicists soon called n the principal quantum number, as they discovered that three other quantum numbers were necessary to fully understand what line spectra were telling them about the state of an electron. One of these was the electron's orbital quantum number, denoted by the letter l, which describes the rotation rate of the electron in its orbit. The second is the magnetic quantum number, denoted by the letter m, which specifies the tilt of the orbit and the direction of the electron's rotation. Think of that orbit as a ring. In the everyday world, you could hold that ring horizontally, vertically, or at any angle in between, and you could spin it at every rate. But in a quantum mechanical world, the orbit can have only certain speeds, depending on the value of l, and it can be tilted only in certain directions, depending on the value of m.

The value of l must always be less than the principal quantum number n, and the value of m

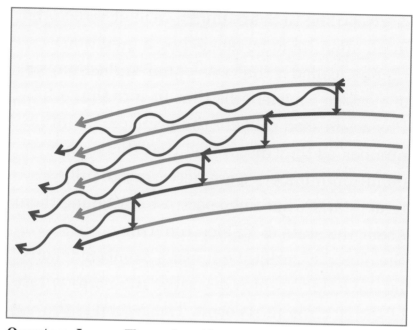

Quantum Jumps. The modern idea of the atom conceives of electrons in "shells" or energy levels rather than orbits. They radiate energy, photons of light, only when they drop to lower energy levels, as shown here. Conversely, they can absorb photons and jump to higher energy levels. Bohr's notion of how this works explained the stability of the Rutherford's model of the atom.

can be between 0 and the value of l. To denote whether an orbit is clockwise or counterclockwise, physicists gave m a minus or plus sign. Thus when n is one, l must be 0. When n equals 2, l and m may both be 0, or l may be 1 while m is 0, plus 1, or minus 1. Finally, just as Earth spins on its axis once per day while orbiting the Sun once a year, an electron also has a spin quantum number, denoted by s, which can only be in one of two states, often called spin up ($s = +\frac{1}{2}$) and spin down ($s = -\frac{1}{2}$).

No two electrons in the same atom can have the same quantum state, the same set of values for n, l, m, and s. Physicists discovered that electrons would fill the quantum states in a predictable order. Some electron arrangements were especially favorable, and larger atoms would use those as a core. Atoms in the same column of the periodic table would have the same pattern of electrons in their outer orbits around different cores. Those outside electrons, called valence electrons, were responsible for an atom's chemical behavior. Quantum mechanics explained why the periodic table is periodic!

Molecular Bonds

Physicists and chemists began speaking of electrons filling shells, which were sets of all the quantum states having the same value of n, subshells, which were smaller parts of those

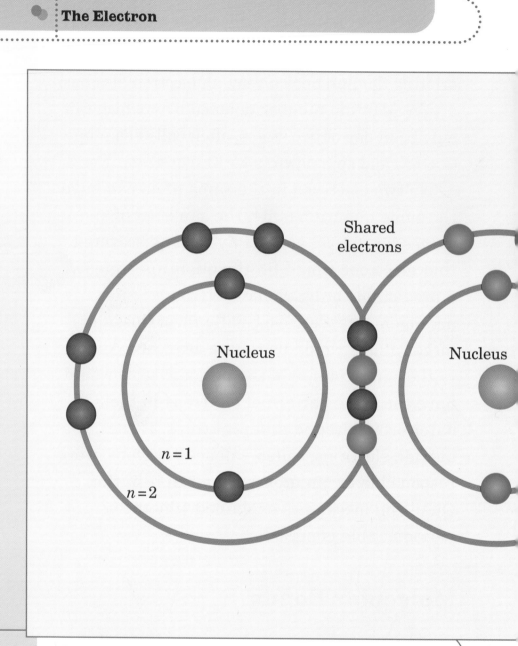

Covalent Bonding. An oxygen molecule (O_2) is formed when two oxygen atoms bond covalently, as shown here. Individually, each oxygen atom has a filled inner shell of two electrons and six of eight permitted electrons in its second or outer shell. By sharing two of those six electrons covalently with each other, both have completely filled outer shells as well.

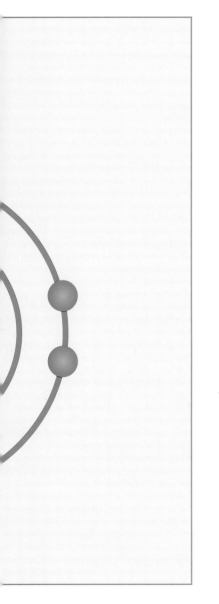

shells having certain values of l. In any column of the periodic table, the core electrons were always in completely filled inner shells and subshells, and the valence electrons were in partially filled outer subshells.

The fewer valence electrons there are, the easier it is to remove them. The elements in column I of the periodic table, sodium and potassium, for example, have only one valence electron, which they give up easily. On the opposite side of the periodic table, the valence electrons are close to filling a subshell and thus have greater attraction not only for each other but also for other electrons that may be nearby. Fluorine and chlorine in column VII, for example, need only one more electron to complete a subshell.

When a chlorine atom and a sodium atom get close to each other, the chlorine snatches the sodium's valence electron, leaving both as electrically charged ions with filled subshells. The positively charged sodium ion and the negatively charged chloride ion experience a strong electrical attraction—an ionic bond— that results in a sodium chloride molecule.

Other kinds of atoms, especially those in the center columns of the periodic table, may join together by sharing rather than exchanging electrons. That is called covalent bonding. For example, a nitrogen atom has five valence electrons in a shell that can hold eight. When two nitrogen atoms share all their valence electrons in a covalent triple bond, it completes the subshells of both. The result is a two-atom nitrogen molecule. Oxygen atoms, too, with six of eight possible electrons in their outer shells, share two each in a covalent double bond to form two-atom oxygen molecules.

Metals get their special properties from a different type of chemical bonding. Each atom shares all of its outer electrons with every other atom, so the metallic bonds are not between pairs of atoms but rather between each atom and the whole. As a result, those shared electrons are only weakly bound to their nearest atom and flow easily to the next one, which explains why metals carry electricity so well. The shared electrons are thus often called conduction electrons.

Metallic bonding also explains why scientists were able to study both the photoelectric effect and cathode rays. If a strip of metal is placed in a beam of ultraviolet light, each photon carries enough energy to free a conduction electron. Likewise, the electric field in a vacuum tube is strong enough to pull some conduction electrons from a heated metal cathode.

Understanding how atoms bond with each other through the sharing or exchanging of electrons advanced the field of chemistry. When scientists finally learned to control electrons, they created a new world of electronic devices unimagined in the early twentieth century.

Chapter Four

Electrons and Electronics

Now the electron has come into commerce, and large workshops and many thousands of workers are employed in its production.

J. J. Thomson

When J. J. Thomson spoke those words in 1934, thirty-seven years after his discovery of the electron, commercial radio was less than fifteen years old but had already transformed the world. Radios of that time were four-foot-high cabinets full of wires and vacuum tubes. Some tubes were as large as today's twelve-ounce soda cans. Inside the tubes were two or more electrodes, including a cathode, a heated filament like the one in a lightbulb. The heat freed conduction electrons, which would flow toward the anode like balls rolling downhill. The greater the voltage, the steeper the hill and the faster the flow of the electric current.

The shape of the other electrodes and their voltage levels would affect that current flow. Small changes in voltage could produce large changes in the current flow through the tube. In that way, the tubes could be used as amplifiers. Passing radio waves would create a weak electric signal in the antenna. The tubes could amplify that signal to power electromagnets, which in turn made smaller magnets vibrate inside paper-cone speakers, producing sound.

Tubes could also act like controllable on-off switches or one-way flow valves for electric currents. Those uses turned out to be ideal for computing, where information of all kinds can be represented in a binary code made up of zeroes and ones. By 1950, improvements in electronics reduced radios to the size of shoe boxes, and a few companies had begun to make room-size computers for the military and a few large corporations.

Then in the 1950s came a breakthrough— the transistor, a device that took advantage of

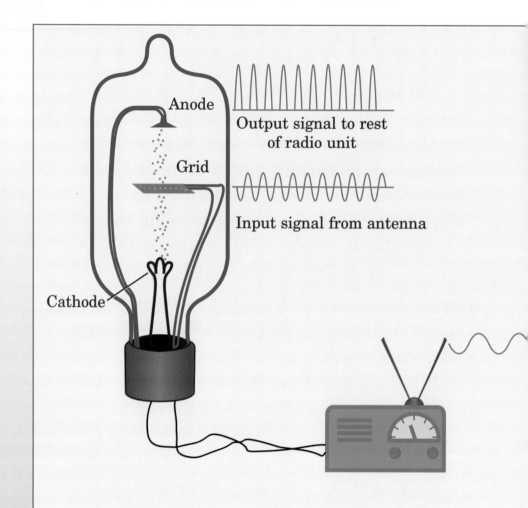

Anode

Output signal to rest of radio unit

Grid

Input signal from antenna

Cathode

A Triode. Many early radios used vacuum tubes, like this triode, so named because it had three electrodes. The cathode, or negative electrode, was a metal filament heated to free some of its electrons, which then flowed toward the anode, or positive electrode. The flow was controlled by the third electrode, a grid, which was connected to an incoming signal. When the grid was more negative, it repelled some of the flowing electrons. When the grid was more positive, it enhanced the flow. Thus it made the input signal stronger or acted as an on-off switch controlled by the input signal.

the way electrons move in materials called semi-conductors, such as silicon. Silicon atoms have four valence electrons, and they join together in a regular arrangement called a crystal by sharing one valence electron with each of four neighboring silicon atoms to fill an eight-electron subshell. Since they are shared among several atoms, the valence electrons can flow easily, but not like in a metal. Atoms are always jiggling, so a few electrons come free. Each free electron leaves behind a "hole," which lasts until another free electron falls in. If you looked inside a semi-conductor connected to a battery, you would see electrons moving from the negative end to the positive end and holes moving in the opposite direction.

To turn a piece of silicon into a transistor, scientists "dope" it by adding small amounts of other substances whose atoms replace silicon atoms in the crystal. If the additive has five valence electrons, like phosphorus, the silicon has extra negatively charged electrons and is called an n-type. Adding a substance that has only three valence electrons such as aluminum results in p-type material with an excess of positively charged holes. The first transistors were n-type and p-type semiconductors joined in a sandwich arrangement. The layers of the sandwich affect electric currents in the same ways as the electrodes in vacuum tubes. Semiconductor devices, however, use much less power, operate much faster, and are also much smaller and cheaper.

By the 1960s, transistor radios were everywhere and computers were becoming more common, but another breakthrough was in the works. Instead of making transistors one at a time, scientists and engineers devised ways to

Scanning Electron Microscope. Microscopes are limited by the wavelength of the energy they use to produce their images. Thus microscopes using visible light cannot produce images of viruses or tiny defects in materials. Electron microscopes can. They take advantage of the quantum mechanical effect that makes particles and waves different aspects of the same thing. This device, called a scanning electron microscope, uses high-energy electrons with very short wavelengths and magnetic lenses to create TV-style images of very small objects.

make hundreds, then thousands, on a single sliver of silicon, connected into integrated circuits, commonly called chips. Today, computer chips with many millions of transistors are

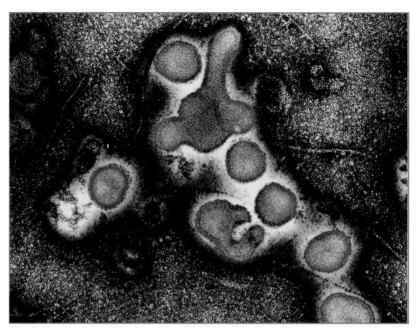

Achoo! This image of the influenza A ("flu") virus was produced by a scanning electron microscope.

everywhere, and companies are continuing to find ways to pack more circuitry into less material at a lower cost.

Seeing with Electrons

Though the quantum world has oddities like fuzzy, wavelike electrons, scientists have learned to take advantage of quantum phenomena to see very small objects. Microscopes cannot produce images of objects smaller than the wavelength of the energy they are using. For example, the wavelength of visible light is smaller than bacteria, but much larger than viruses. Yet you have probably seen images of viruses. Those images were created by electron microscopes.

Electron microscopes are possible because high-energy electrons have very short wavelengths, and their paths can be bent by magnets. Scientists have built electron microscopes with magnetic lenses, and they use them to study not only viruses, but also new "high-tech" materials.

Transistors on integrated circuits are getting smaller all the time, and the same is true of many other useful structures. People working in the important fields of materials science and materials engineering need to be able to check out how the chemistry and structure of those materials vary from place to place. Electron microscopes not only produce images, but they also create X-rays that can be used to identify the atoms in the tiny regions that the electrons hit.

Another kind of imaging uses a different kind of electron. You may have read or heard about antimatter, especially if you're a fan of science fiction. But antimatter is real. Every subatomic particle has its antiparticle with the same mass but an opposite charge. If the two particles meet, they annihilate each other, producing two very energetic photons (gamma rays) going in opposite directions.

The electron's antiparticle is the positron. Just as many radioactive elements produce beta rays, which are really electrons, a few produce positrons. A medical device called a positron emission tomography (PET) scanner produces images of the living brain that identify brain damage and abnormalities better than any other method. A new device for materials science uses positrons to identify microscopic defects in metallic crystal structures that signal the very earliest signs of metal fatigue.

The wavelike nature of electrons even makes it possible for scientists to observe individual atoms or molecules with devices called scanning tunneling microscopes (STMs) and atomic force microscopes (AFMs). Both devices use a small sharp needle that moves just above the surface being measured. The needle is so close to the surface that the wave functions of electrons at its tip extend into the material. That means that each electron has a small probability of crossing the gap as part of a "tunneling" current, so named because the electrons seem to tunnel through an energy barrier rather than go over it. By scanning the needle back and forth across the surface, an STM produces an image of the atoms on the surface from the varying intensity of the tunneling current.

An AFM keeps the tunneling current constant by allowing the needle to move up and down on a springlike device as it scans the surface. In effect, it "feels" the surface bumps as it moves along. Scientists are now finding ways to pick up and move single atoms or molecules using devices like AFMs. What technological wonders will that ability lead us to? No one knows, but the road we will take to get there will surely be the same one J. J. Thomson followed to discover the electron. As Thomson said so colorfully in 1934, "Any new discovery contains the germ of a new industry . . . Take the hair of the dog that bit you, and go in for more and more research."

• Glossary

atom The smallest bit of matter than can be identified as a certain chemical element.

anode and cathode The positive and negative terminals of a battery or pieces of metal (electrodes) attached to them.

cathode ray A beam of electrons that flows from the cathode in a glass tube from which most of the air has been removed.

compound A substance made of only one kind of molecule that consists of more than one kind of atom. For example, water is made of molecules that contain two atoms of hydrogen and one atom of oxygen.

covalent, ionic, and metallic bonds Different ways in which atoms can join together by sharing or exchanging some of their electrons.

electromagnetic wave A form of energy resulting from the interrelationship of changing electric and magnetic fields that flows through space at the speed of light.

electromagnetism A fundamental force of nature, or property of matter and energy, that includes electricity, magnetism, and electromagnetic waves, such as light.

electrometer A device that measures the amount of electrical charge.

electronics A field of technology that takes advantage of the ability to control the motion of electrons.

electron microscopy A technology that uses the wavelike or quantum mechanical properties of electrons to produce images of very small objects or features.

element A substance made of only one kind of atom.

energy level One of many values of energy that an electron can have in an atom.

molecule The smallest bit of matter that can be identified as a certain chemical compound.

photon A particle that carries electromagnetic energy, such as light energy.

positron The antiparticle of an electron. If an electron and positron meet, they annihilate each other and produce pure energy in the form of two high-energy photons traveling in opposite directions.

quantum mechanics A field of physics that deals with the relationships between matter and energy that accounts for the dual wave-particle nature of both.

shells and subshells Particularly stable sets of energy levels in atoms that electrons tend to occupy.

spectrum The mixture of colors contained within a beam of light, or the band produced when those colors are spread out by a prism or other device that separates the colors from each other.

tunneling A quantum mechanical phenomenon in which, due to its wavelike properties, a particle crosses a barrier, as if through a tunnel, when it lacks sufficient energy to get over the top.

ultraviolet catastrophe A breakdown in Max Planck's mathematical description of the spectrum of hot bodies that required him to devise the idea of the quantum.

valence electron One of the electrons outside an atom's filled shells or subshells. Valence electrons are responsible for the atom's chemical properties.

wave function The quantum mechanical description that expresses the wavelike properties of a particle.

For More Information

Organizations

Lederman Science Center
Fermilab MS 777
Box 500
Batavia, IL 60510
Web site: http://www-ed.fnal.gov/ed_lsc.html
This museum is an outstanding place to discover
the science and history of subatomic particles. It
is located at the Fermi National Accelerator
Laboratory (Fermilab) outside of Chicago.

Magazines

American Scientist
P.O. Box 13975
Research Triangle Park, NC 27709-3975
Web site: http://www.americanscientist.org

New Scientist (U.S. offices of British magazine)
275 Washington Street, Suite 290
Newton, MA 02458
Web site: http://www.newscientist.com

Science News
1719 N Street NW
Washington, DC 20036
Web site: http://www.sciencenews.org

Scientific American
415 Madison Avenue
New York, NY 10017
Web site: http://www.sciam.com

Web Sites

Due to the changing nature of Internet links, the Rosen Publishing Group, Inc., has developed an online list of Web sites related to the subject of this book. This site is updated regularly. Please use this link to access the list:

http://www.rosenlinks.com/lsap/elec

For Further Reading

Bortz, Fred. *Techno-Matter: The Materials Behind the Marvels.* Brookfield, CT: Twenty-First Century Books, 2001.

Bridgman, Roger. *Electronics* (Eyewitness Books). New York: Dorling Kindersley, Inc., 2000.

Close, Frank, Michael Marten, and Christine Sutton. *The Particle Odyssey: A Journey to the Heart of Matter.* New York: Oxford University Press, 2002.

Cooper, Christopher. *Matter* (Eyewitness Books). New York: Dorling Kindersley, Inc., 2000.

Henderson, Harry, and Lisa Yount. *The Scientific Revolution.* San Diego: Lucent Books, 1996.

Narins, Brigham, ed. *Notable Scientists from 1900 to the Present.* Farmington Hills, MI: The Gale Group, 2001.

Bibliography

Close, Frank, Michael Marten, and Christine Sutton. *The Particle Odyssey: A Journey to the Heart of Matter*. New York: Oxford University Press, 2002.

Cropper, William H. *Great Physicists: The Life and Times of Leading Physicists from Galileo to Hawking*. New York: Oxford University Press, 2001.

Nobel Foundation. *Nobel Lectures in Physics, 1901–1921*. River Edge, NJ: World Scientific Publishing Company, 1998.

Physics Today, October 1997 (special edition on the centennial of the electron).

Young, Hugh D., and Roger A. Freedman. *University Physics: Extended Version with Modern Physics*. Reading, MA: Addison-Wesley Publishing Co., 2000.

Index

About the Author

Award-winning children's author Fred Bortz spent the first twenty-five years of his working career as a physicist, gaining experience in fields as varied as nuclear reactor design, automobile engine control systems, and science education. He earned his Ph.D. at Carnegie-Mellon University, where he also worked in several research groups from 1979 through 1994. He has been a full-time writer since 1996.

Photo Credits

Cover, pp. 10, 12–13, 14, 17, 18–19, 22, 30, 32, 38, 40–41, 46–47 by Thomas Forget; p. 7 © Science Photo Library; p. 9 © Courtesy of the Archives, California Institute of Technology ; p. 20 © Prof. Peter Fowler/Science Photo Library; p. 25 © Margrethe Bohr Collection/American Institute of Physics/Science Photo Library; p. 35 © Novosti/Science Photo Library; p. 36 © W. F. Meggers Collection/American Institute of Physics/Science Photo Library; p. 49 © Colin Cuthbert/Science Photo Library; p. 50 © Mike Miller/Science Photo Library.

Designer: Thomas Forget; Editor: Jake Goldberg